The Nature of Our Minds

The Nature of Our Minds

Written by Shaley Ronan

All artwork created by Amber Haney

# The Nature of Our Minds

Dedicated to everyone I met in this world. You made me into the person I am today, and I will forever be grateful for that.

Words to describe living are hard to find.

All the years are comprised of up and downs constantly colliding.

# Contents

# Discovery

# Rain

Water droplets fall from the sky,

flowers yell with excitement.

People scream in sorrow,

but little do they know,

that what makes one grieve,

could make something else grow.

# River Bank

She would walk down to the river,

day and night.

Quiet and peaceful,

little commotion in sight.

She would sit down on the side of the river bank,

glance into the water,

to see her reflection between the ripples.

Wondering about life,

because maybe if she jumped in,

she wouldn't come back up alive.

# Waves

Sharp cold crashing waves.

They rush over her,

they drag her under,

until she reaches the bottom.

The ground with sand,

coarsely rubbing against her skin.

Getting into her mouth and eyes,

leaving a harsh residue all over her.

But she sees sunlight,

and she rises.

The oxygen filling her lungs,

seagulls over her head making their beautiful call.

The warmth of the sun heating her entire body,

a moment of pure bliss and simple tranquility.

But just then another wave comes,

and this time, maybe she won't rise.

# Leaving the Shadow

Shadow...

Now she's the slut he told everyone about,

bragging, changing, manipulating the reality of what really happened.

She got stripped of her clothes, stripped of her trust, stripped of her youth.

But to him, she was just a check off of his list.

She had sleepless nights, while he had rest.

She had tears in her eyes while he ran around as happy as could be.

He ruined her, but he didn't care.


She knew she had to face it, but repressing feelings was easier.

She knew she had to forgive him and move on,

but how could she forgive him?

She tried to figure it out, tried to find a reason why he would do this to her, but she couldn't.

She couldn't erase the night.

She could wipe of the dirt, but the bruises remained.

The scratches on her skin would heal but the guilt, the shame, the unworthiness stayed.

Danger was everywhere.

Hands felt the same, voices sounded similar, the demons always lingered.

How could she feel safe when every man who touched her reminded her of him?

It followed her everywhere.

It wasn't human, but appeared to be so.

It didn't talk, but lurk.

It didn't love, but hate.

It didn't heal, but destroy.

It was a shadow, so dark and so cold.

Light...

Healing didn't happen overnight.

There was months of sorrow,

months of hate,

months upon months of darkness.

She woke up one day

and realized it was her time.

Her time to heal, her time to grow.

She looked at the world in a whole new light.

It wasn't dark,

it was dim.

Darkness is always there, but there was hope.

She woke up that day new.

She wasn't a young girl,

she was a women.

With more passion in her fingertips than people had throughout their whole body.

Though her mind was damaged,

her soul was kind.

She had drive and ambition to take her pain and to turn it into beauty.

To take her darkness and turn it into light.

She was reborn.

She surrounded herself with positive people,

met the most loving and caring souls on this earth.

She was happy.

She was free.

Though she still remember the night, but found forgiveness in herself.

Not for him, but for her.

She forgave herself for thinking it was her fault.

That maybe if she didn't wear shorts that night it wouldn't of happened.

She forgave herself for hating every inch of her skin that he touched.

She forgave herself for the exhaustion she had from all the restless nights.

Because none of this mess was because of clothes or action.

It was a shadow,

but she was the sun.

More powerful than ever before with a fire in her soul,

burning with fight.

With the flames, the love, and the faith in this universe,

she ran, and ran and ran.

She had left the shadow.

# To the Girl in the Mirror

She is not the girl whose life was always filled with sunshine.

She is also not the girl whose world was constantly rained on.

She isn't flawless in her face or in her actions.

Everyone makes mistakes,

and she was no exception.


She cries often,

even though she hates her cheeks being soaked in tears.

She knows she will be taken advantage of in this world,

but still throws her heart out into the universe.


She spread her soul across the Earth,

because people who respect her love will stay.


She loves her life,

even though sometimes she feels taken over by it.

Refresh

# Escape

Caged up and confused,

no where to go.

She reached out,

and scraped up her words.

'I am trapped" she says.

They turn around and laugh.


It is all fun and games,

until she finds the key.

# Moon

The moon is always changing,

day by day,

night by night.

Though it is not always fully there,

the moon is always in the sky.


She was the moon.

Not full everyday.

Not out in the open for everyone to see and admire.

The constant changing and evolving that she has to go through,

is what her life was made of.

But the moon is always the moon in all of its phases.

# The Boy Next Door

He was wild.

Something she always wanted,

but never could grasp.


She lived for the late nights.

The hours of talking until 4 am.

The risk of being caught.

The excitement of the unknown.


He was her rebellion.

Read When: You Feel Alone

1. Everyone will be alone at some point throughout their lives and in their day-to-day. It is nothing to be afraid of. There is a difference between having time to yourself and feeling lonely. No one should ever feel lonely. There are so many people in this world to spend time with and create the best memories with.

2. There is no shame in having some alone time. This time teaches you how to be your own rock. It teaches you how to take care of yourself, and how to figure things out by yourself. This will give you the strength to move up in the world, which is a beautiful thing.

3. If you are alone, and feel lonely, don't worry. Loneliness can come, it is normal and okay. Keep in your heart that there are so many people who love and care about you. Even if they are physically not there with you, it does not mean that they aren't rooting for you. Take the loneliness, and do something you enjoy. You can go and get some good food. Or put on a movie and some comfy clothes. Or even go on a drive and jam to some of your favorite songs. Be by yourself and enjoy it. You are the person you will always have every second of your life with, so have fun with that person.

# Begin Again

We are the trees

Growing and blooming.

Burned down,

to then be replanted again.


Our leaves fall and we are reborn.

We begin again.

# Confidence

She never been a skinny girl,

but she was one to turn heads.

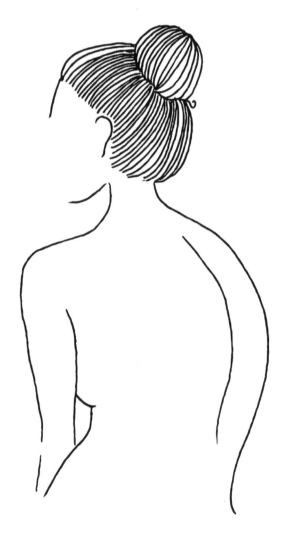

# Slow Down

Growing up fast made her motived to climb.

Every mountain top,

never seemed to high to reach.


But there comes a time,

were she stops at the top,

and breathes in the fresh air.

She does not need to keep climbing,

but just enjoy the mountain she is on.

All of the potential in her life.

The views from high above.

The pride of making it so far already.


There is no shame in stopping and enjoying where you are in life.

Read When: You are Overwhelmed or Worrying

1. Identify what is making you worry or concerned. Sometimes everything in life may feel like it is crumbling. Maybe the world feels like it is against you. I promise you, it is not. Everything happens for a reason. List down your worries in the notes on your phone, a piece of paper, anything. Releasing it into the world can help to get it off of your mind.

2. Worrying and feeling overwhelmed can come from a lack of control. It is normal to want to be able to control everything in your life. You cannot control other people, their thoughts, or their actions. You have to let go of how other people have control on your life. Control yourself first. You have to be the most important person in your life.

3. Stop thinking of what other people think of you. It can be difficult to not think about other people's opinions but life is so much more rewarding if you are living it for you. Do what makes you happy. You are not on this Earth to please everyone around you. Take control of your own happiness.

4. You may not be able to have everything you want in life all at once. That is okay. Sometimes life gets in the way and you have to readjust to make sure you don't run yourself out. Working hard and making strides is important, but make sure you save time to breathe and enjoy your life.

# Last Week

<u>Sunday</u>

She wondered the streets,

hoping for a sign that she will be okay.

<u>Monday</u>

She slept past her alarm,

a late start that doesn't even matter.

<u>Tuesday</u>

She fell apart,

she should be used to that by now.

<u>Wednesday</u>

 She was hopeful,

to only be let down.

## Thursday

She rushed around;

commotion was a good distraction.


## Friday

She exhaled her sorrows,

in attempt to re-balance her system.


## Saturday

She drowned her wounds inside,

disinfecting the pain.

# Spiral

# Collision

Her mind is a field.

Everlasting and open,

with a clear view of everything ahead.

She wish she could stay in that field,

but her heart gets lost.

Tangled up in the weeds.

Confused by the dandelions.

Clashed with the tiny ants that lay in between the grass.

She grew from the crowding.


The head and the heart collide,

but it is no reason to lose balance.

# Stage Fright

She remembers her first play.

Acting came so natural,

so she became one.

An actress always trying to please an audience.

Encore after encore.

When the lights turn back on.

she is blinded.

She is lost in the crowd,

no one sees her.

She is hidden behind the curtains of fake smiles

and 'I am okay"s .

When the audience is gone,

she takes off the mask,

removes the script and

all she needs is not to perform.

Off stage is uncomfortable,

but it is better to be speechless than have lines

memorized.

# I Need Aloe

Comparison is the devil.

They took his flames,

and lit her up when her skin was already burned.

# Ice

She freezes when she is in danger.

Her body stiff and cold,

hands of the shadow push her to the ground,

and just in seconds,

she is frozen.

Maybe if her legs could move,

she could run.

Maybe if her hands could clench into a fist,

she could fight back.

Her mouth moves,

but her words mean nothing to the shadow.


Frozen.

Pure Ice.

Lost in the mist of a shadow.

# The Fall Back

She thought she left the shadow.

Clouds came and gone.

Memories blocked, but not forgotten.

Repression and freedom sometimes go hand and hand.

The most gentle of hands cannot hold her tight enough,

that she can be free.

She is ready to not even know what a shadow is anymore,

but that what she knows in her life the most.

# The Shadows

She knows the shadows well,

for she met them twice before.

Only sixteen and seventeen years old,

haunted by two shadows,

that she wants to escape.

She just wishes that she could protect herself.

# Numb

She wakes up,

with no sun in her eyes.

She gets out of bed,

to brush her teeth with flavorless paste.

She puts on a gray sweatshirt and jeans,

nothing to be seen.

She walks down the hall,

silence is everywhere.

She sits in class,

to learn that the clock ticks,

and the wall is white.

She sips on her coffee,

to awaken nothing.

Read When: You Feel Hopeless

1. It is easy to lose hope. It is easy to stay still. It is easy to blame everyone else instead of hunting down the answers that lie within yourself. Do some soul searching. What really makes you happy? What makes you sad? What can you do to prevent the sad thoughts from ruining the good times?

2. Realize your worth in this world. The laugh that you might hate, brings people joy. Genuine laughter is the best laughter. The smile that may be crooked, is the most beautiful feature to others. The most hated parts of yourself, can be seen as the greatest aspects to someone else. Confidence will get you so far. Flaws are opinions, not facts. Believe that you can be both attractive and strong. You can be goofy and sexy. You can be cute and serious. You can and are everything and more.

3. Trust the timing of your life. Write down the best things in your life that has happened to you. Whether it is ten amazing times, or just one fun night, read and remember that moment or all of the moments. Imagine how many more amazing things you can experience in this world. It is a lot easier to live in this world if you think your best days haven't happened yet.

4. Life is all about perceptive. Have faith in the universe, even when it is the hardest thing to do.

# To All the Broken Boys

Life has no ruling of who to ruin.

Who to bruise.

Who to challenge and push to the end of insanity.

To all the broken boys,

you are allowed to be scared, overwhelmed, and depressed.

Everyone is wounded.

You are not an exception

to hide behind the untrue rulings of masculinity.

# Lost

She is sorry that she lost herself.

She is sorry that she cannot verbalize anything correctly.

She is sorry that there were a thousand needles piling onto her haystack that

it shortly collapsed.

She lost herself but,

she misses herself more than anything.

Which makes everyone realize,

that she will find her way back home.

# Disappointment

She can capture an ocean,

but they wanted a river.

She is blooming like a birch tree,

tall and strong,

but they wanted a clover.

She grew up so fast that turning back is not an option.

She shouts into the void,

praying and looking for answers.


They do not believe that the void exists.

She's sorry that they don't have that faith.

# Awake

In the dark ibis.

Wide awake.

For the endless hours of darkness taunt her

with the choking of silence

and the walls closing in.

The silence performs tricks on her mind

and the walls jump forward as the

nothingness of the night,

becomes so loud

that she is deafened.

She wants the quiet whisper of the sun,

to rise and numb the roar of the night.

She lays,

for hours on end.

Replaying nightmares in her mind as the darkness floods into her brain.

She is stuck in the night

and the days she can't erase.

# Bliss

How blessed is she that her life is so beautiful?

For the second she falls asleep,

she cannot wait to wake up.

# Youth

She wants to remember her years growing up,

as hazy late nights,

as spontaneous adventures,

as moments that feel like they are meant for movie screens.

# I Will Always Admire Daises

Gentle and wild,

all at the same time.

That's why they are her favorite flower.

A bouquet of the most soft petals,

with vibrant centers and the strongest of stems.

The most simple example of grace.

But a bouquet of daises would be so dull,

if they didn't come from him.

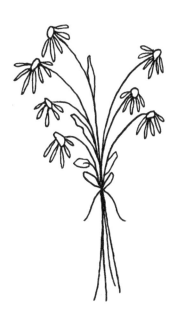

# I Like You

Feeling safe in a world that she is terrified of

is when she knew it was real.

It is not superficial.

It is not simple.

It is the sweetest glimpse of freedom

It is walking into the unknown with her hand held tight.

When she says ' I like you',

it is because of the beautiful security that makes her know that

she is untouched.

# I Love You

Sometimes the most beautiful things in this world cannot be explained.

She doesn't exactly know how to verbalize it.

She loves him like a tiger hunts.

Intense and natural,

fast enough that sometimes he can't even see it.

She remembers him like she tells a story.

Focused not on the big picture,

but rather detailed in every single second.

She misses him like a desert misses rain.

Knowing what everything could be,

longing for a single droplet of water to come.

# Passion

His hair swirling like dandelion seeds in the wind

His lips sweet like a garden blossoming in harvest.

His tongue smooth and sharp as ice.

His hands gentle and warm, but tight.

His teeth firm and light.

His purpose to love and please,

in the most gentle and rough ways.

# 5 A.M

She always woke up randomly through the night.

Maybe her mind was too wild to be put to rest.

Maybe she was so exhausted that sleep couldn't even help.

Maybe she was so full of life, that going to bed seemed pointless.

But there was that time she woke up,

at 5 a.m.

He was there with her.

He pulled her into his arms.

At that 5 a.m.,

she knew that her life would never be the same.

# Why I Stopped Reading Novels

She used to read stories about falling in love.

She used to read stories about traveling,

to the most breathtaking locations in the world.

She used to read stories about meeting new people,

in the most unexpected places.

She used to read every night.

But when she found love,

the love stories became boring.

When she took a flight across the sea,

traveling in words seemed pointless.

When she went grocery shopping,

and talked to a stranger for thirty minutes in an aisle,

reading about meeting people that don't exist felt useless.


She stopped reading about everything she wanted,

because it was right there in front of her.

"Never let anything ruin your kind soul'

That is what her mother always told her

No matter where she goes,

she will always root for one of the strongest women she knows.

That is what sisters do.

# Butterflies

She remembers her grandmother in butterflies.

There is no surprise how often they appear in her life.

For every big day.

For every sad thought.

For every stressful moment.

A butterfly flutters onto the grass beside her.

A reminder that no matter where her path takes her,

winding roads,

rocky mountains,

or wide open fields.

A butterfly will follow behind.

# Angels

She is not the girl who went to church every Sunday.

She never read the Bible or frankly even held it.

She doesn't know how to pray,

and maybe doesn't even want to.

She believes there is something.

Some higher power to give her hope.

But she hates the idea of heaven and hell,

and lists of sins she must stay away from.

That this concept of redemption is her only way of living.

She loves her neighbors,

and believes there is no good to be found in evil.

The division between the Devil and God is blurred.


But when she looks into his eyes,

she would be insane,

to think angels don't exist.

Read When: You are Falling In Love

1. Embrace the butterflies. I know it is easy to be afraid, and maybe a little hesitant. But fully take in all of the good feelings when you are falling in love. Embracing it makes it so much more enjoyable than running away from it.

2. Try your best not to worry about the future. No one can predict what will happen in days, months, or years down the road. Do not worry about 'what ifs' or a plan ahead. Just enjoy every moment you have with that person. Falling in love is one of the greatest gifts in this world, live in the moment of it all.

3. It is hard not to spend every second with the person you love. It is still very important to make sure you take time for yourself and other people you care about. Friends and family are just as important to make new memories with. It is important you still keep in touch with other people you value in your life.

4. Never let the person you love feel taken for granted. It is so easy to show how much you love someone, just as much as it is easy to show that you don't. When you are in a relationship do little things for them that show how much you truly care. This can be the smallest things like a surprise gift, a nice dinner or even an extra sweet text or phone call. The little things are really what matters to show someone you love them. Never let a day go by that the person you love feels unappreciated.

5. Falling in love is the most crazy, confusing, beautiful feeling one could ever experience. It can be hard. Every relationship will have their bumps in the road, and there is no perfect or right way to love someone. At the end of the day, the most important thing is to just love foolishly, deeply and as hard as you can.

# Stars

The clusters of glow.

The constellations of light.

Each tiny cosmic glimmers,

shined through that night.

After all that time,

they met eye to eye.

She'll forever be grateful,

for that night.

The night all the stars aligned.

# 11:11

She wishes she met him at a different time.

Though she doesn't regret a second of time together,

she just wishes for a better time.

A time when she could look herself in the mirror,

and stand tall.

The time that she could take anything on.

She has that fight,

for she lives in nightmares,

but still sees the beauty in the world.

Though some days the girl in the mirror is unrecognizable.

The twinkle in her eyes faded.

The spark that makes her glow turned to a dim beam.

She wishes that she could met him again.

When he could stare at a girl so familiar,

yet he knows nothing about.

Someone who he knows he could understand,

but has so much to learn.

Someone that he could love,

because he have given her so much love before.

She wants those magic days back.

But the days will feel like bliss without her frustration,

without tears,

without doubt.

The days she could honestly say that she has so much faith in the universe,

that she has nothing to worry about.

The days that she can not be bothered by the people not believing in all that she is.

The days that she can live in the moment and just act her age,

with no concern of what is to come.

She can't wait for those days.

For the best days of her life haven't happened yet.

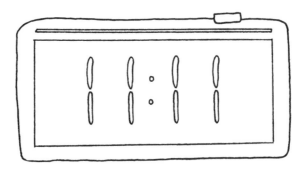

# Italia

She found herself in Rome.

Surrounded by people she known for years,

and met people for the first time,

to never see again.


 The beautiful thing about Italy,

for the moments are so rare,

that they carry a weight of memory,

yet float so fearlessly.

With each round,

and every song that was from years ago.

That the same music that played at her middle school dance

was playing in a club years later around the world.

That is the beautiful thing about Italy,

it reminds her how far she has come.

Italy had no commitment.

The boy who she glazed her lips against his cheek,

had no hope for her coming back.


The people she met,

had no vision to be united again.


That is the beautiful thing about Italy.

 No standards to follow or comply.

Just snippets of time to hold on to.

# Super Glue

She wishes her words could single handedly heal all the wounds in the world.

That her lips could glaze every broken heart to give them love once more.

That her gentle hands could erase the bruises of the beaten.

That her arms could wrap around every alone soul to give them company.

That the vowels and consonants creating words and lines,

with the twenty six letters,

could touch and heal the broken.

But her words are like super glue.

The spoken tongue of beliefs that can't heal but to be applied,

by the soul who wants to be better.

She can't fix the battles or wounds,

but she can give the world super glue.

For the universe to apply to all the shattered pieces,

all the shards of pain,

for then the people to place back together,

to be whole again.

Farewell

# Death Bed

She rested her head in between the pillows of a broken promise /

Maybe she was a fool to believe she would live out her biggest dreams.

A false hope / That girls in their teenage years don't die,

but death flashed before her eyes / as she laid into her death bed

to see the truth about life.


She couldn't paint mountain tops / or turn rivers into gold.

She couldn't get married / or build a family of her own.

She couldn't get her dream job / or go on her dream vacation.

These shattered dreams are nothing compared to what her life was /

short-lived but not lack luster.


Death is seeing the night sky for the first time /

The soothing kiss of the stars that she saw in so many people's eyes /

The connection bonded through constellations.

Her lovers and friends are the stars that scatter the earth we all walk on

/ she realized she wasted time in darkness that took away from the light /

As she rested into her death bed,

pulled over the covers

and regretfully said


/ 'goodnight'/

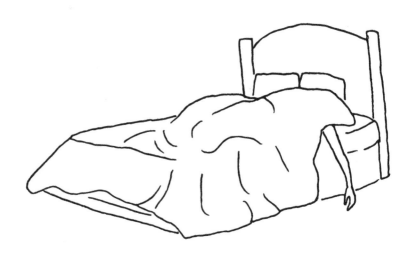

# After I Go

A monument of flowers.

Smooth granite symbolizing something so lively,

for someone who is dead

Stone created to show the most delicate and elegant parts of nature.

My family knew how to represent me.

My parents spend hours, days, relentlessly carving love and morn into

every petal, leaf and stem.

I am a flower garden now,

that's how I lay.

A stone garden of daisies,

so gentle and warm,

resting near a pond.

My husband leaves daisies with me every day,

I wish I could say 'thank you'.

My sister comes to just talk.

I wish I could give her a response.

An older couple walks through the park every morning and looks at the garden.

I wish I could say 'hello',

I always loved meeting new people.

Just like when I was alive,

I got damaged.

The flowers got weathered by the wind,

ruined from the rain,

slaughtered from the snow.

My family comes after every storm,

trying to rebuild the garden.

After years of abrasion,

it never looks the same.


The natural world takes a toll on people.

CPSIA information can be obtained
at www.ICGtesting.com
Printed in the USA
BVHW062208120720
583530BV00006B/441